Vegetarian Curry Cookbook

50 Delicious Vegetarian Curry Recipes
That Everyone Can Enjoy

By
BookSumo Press
All rights reserved

Published by
http://www.booksumo.com

ENJOY THE RECIPES?
KEEP ON COOKING
WITH 6 MORE FREE COOKBOOKS!

Visit our website and simply enter your email address to join the club and receive your 6 cookbooks.

http://booksumo.com/magnet

LEGAL NOTES

All Rights Reserved. No Part Of This Book May Be Reproduced Or Transmitted In Any Form Or By Any Means. Photocopying, Posting Online, And / Or Digital Copying Is Strictly Prohibited Unless Written Permission Is Granted By The Book's Publishing Company. Limited Use Of The Book's Text Is Permitted For Use In Reviews Written For The Public.

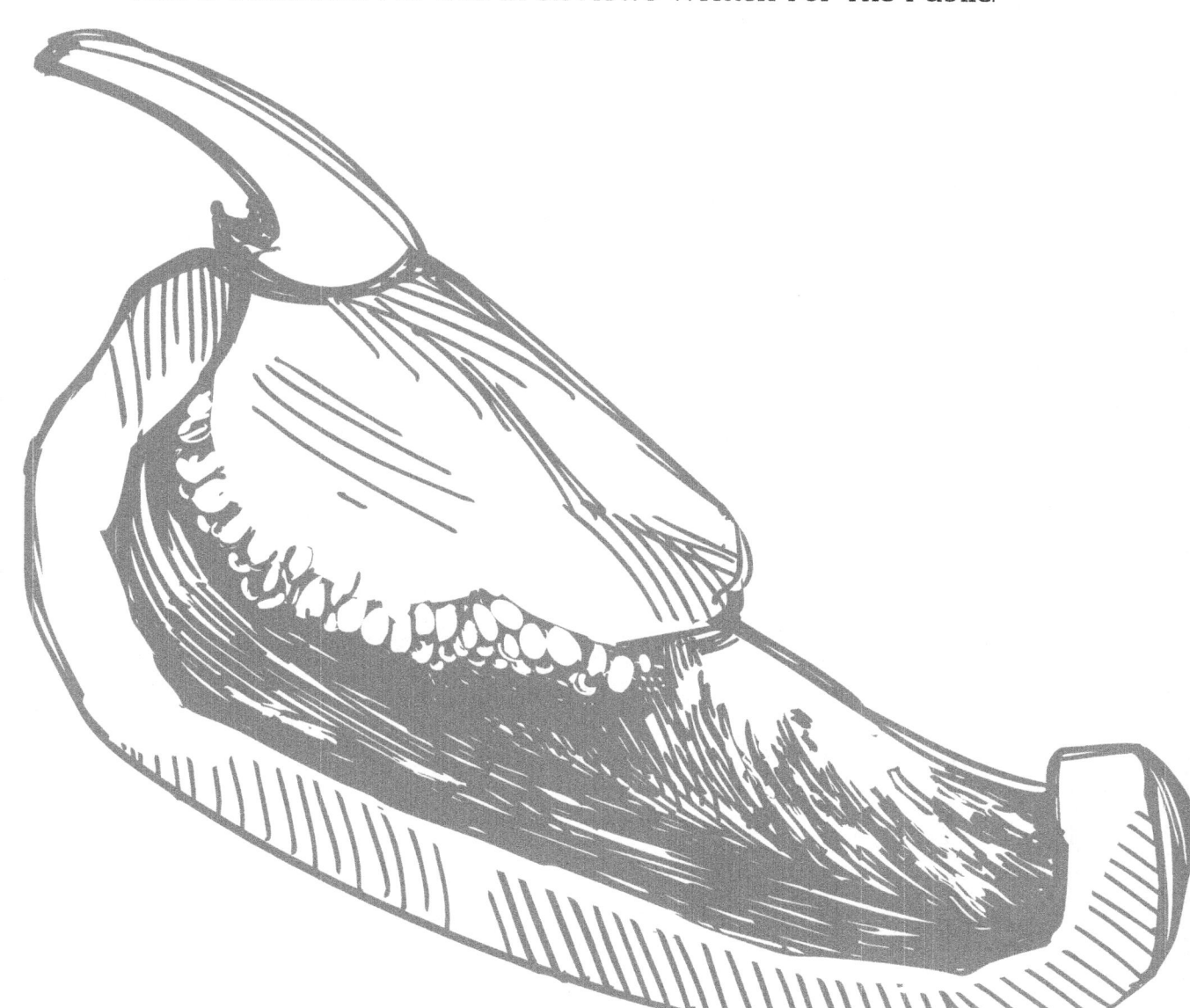

Table of Contents

Ethiopian Curry 7

A Vegetarian's Dream 8

Kidney Beans, Lentils, and Garbanzo Curry 9

Vietnamese Curry 10

Crock Pot Curry 11

American Yukon Curry 12

Asian Curried Coleslaw 13

Hyderabadi Curry 14

Madras Veggie Curry 15

Restaurant Style Okra 16

Microwave Okra Curry 17

Simply Lentils Curry 18

Aunties' Chickpea Dinner 19

American Curry Corn 20

Caterer's Curry Soup 21

Summer Potluck Curry Salad 22

Seema's Delight 23

Vegetarian Chicken Curry 24

Quinoa Masala 25

Microwave Pea Curry 26

Spicy Squash Curry 27

Full Indian Curry 28

Curried Rice Salad 30

Authentic Jamaican Curry 31

North Indian Curried Cauliflower 32

Rustic Thai Mushroom Curry 33

Microwave Broccoli Curry 34

Saturday Night Curry 35

October's Apple Curry 36

Lunch Box Soup Curry 37

Whole Grain Curry 38

Vegetarian Curry Japanese Style 39

Curry Salad 41

South East Asian All Ingredient Curry 42

Punjabi Greens Curry 43

Easy Veggie Curry Soup from Vietnam 44

Vegetarian Curry Sri Lankan Style 45

Peanut Thai Curry 47

Traditional North Indian Beans Curry 48

Veggie Curry Burgers 50

Potato Curry for Winter 52

Thai Tofu Curry 53

Western Moroccan Curry 54

Squash, Eggplant, and Tomato Curry from Brazil 55

Aromatic Kenyan Curry 56

Cauliflower, Pumpkin, and Lentil Curry 57

Peas, Zucchini, and Cabbage Curry 58

Microwave Carrot Curry 59

Odia Veggie Curry 60

Caribbean Country Curry 61

Traditional Indian Curry Paste 62

Green Curry Paste (Thailand Style) 63

Ethiopian Curry

Prep Time: 25 mins
Total Time: 2 hr 5 mins

Servings per Recipe: 4
Calories   226 kcal
Fat   8.9 g
Carbohydrates   33.6g
Protein   6.7 g
Cholesterol   0 mg
Sodium   502 mg

Ingredients

2 tbsp olive oil
1/2 onion, diced
2 cloves garlic, minced
1 tbsp ground cumin
2 tbsp curry powder
1 (15 oz.) can garbanzo beans (chickpeas), undrained
1/2 red bell pepper, diced
1/2 turnip, peeled and diced
1 C. corn kernels
1/2 (15 oz.) can tomato sauce
1 pinch crushed red pepper flakes
1 pinch salt
1 pinch cracked black pepper

Directions

1. In a large pan, heat the olive oil on medium heat and sauté the onion, garlic, cumin and curry powder for about 5 minutes.
2. Add the garbanzo beans, red bell pepper, turnip, corn, tomato sauce, red pepper flakes, salt and black pepper and bring to a boil on medium-high heat.
3. Reduce the heat to medium-low and simmer, covered for about 1 1/2-2 hours.

A VEGETARIAN'S
Dream

🥣 Prep Time: 15 mins
🕐 Total Time: 50 mins

Servings per Recipe: 4
Calories 253 kcal
Fat 8.8 g
Carbohydrates 38.4g
Protein 8.8 g
Cholesterol 0 mg
Sodium 511 mg

Ingredients

2 tbsp olive oil
1 tsp cumin seeds
3 whole cloves
1 white onion, halved and thinly sliced
3 oz. tomato paste
2 tbsp curry powder
1 tbsp all-purpose flour
1 tbsp ground turmeric
1 tsp garlic powder
1 tsp ground ginger
1 tsp dried basil

1 pinch ground allspice
1 pinch salt
3 C. warm water
1 (15 oz.) can garbanzo beans, drained
1/3 red bell pepper, chopped
2 C. fresh green beans, trimmed
1 C. frozen peas
1 tsp rice wine vinegar
salt and ground black pepper to taste

Directions

1. In a large pan, heat the oil on medium-high heat and sauté the cumin seeds and cloves for about 30 seconds.
2. Discard the cloves.
3. Add the onion to the pot and sauté for about 5 minutes.
4. In a bowl, mix together the tomato paste, curry powder, flour, turmeric, garlic powder, ginger, basil, allspice and salt.
5. Stir in 1 C. of the warm water.
6. Stir in the tomato mixture and additional water and cook till a sauce like mixture forms.
7. Add the garbanzo beans and bell pepper and stir to combine.
8. Reduce the heat and simmer for about 5 minutes.
9. Stir in the green beans, peas, rice wine vinegar, salt and black pepper and simmer for about 20-25 minutes, stirring occasionally.

Kidney Beans Lentils, and Garbanzo Curry

Prep Time: 15 mins
Total Time: 1 hr 25 mins

Servings per Recipe: 8
Calories   208 kcal
Fat   4.7 g
Carbohydrates   35.9 g
Protein   8.7 g
Cholesterol   0 mg
Sodium   298 mg

Ingredients

- 2 tbsp olive oil
- 1 large white onion, chopped
- 1/2 C. dry lentils
- 2 cloves garlic, minced
- 3 tbsp curry powder
- 1 tsp ground cumin
- 1 pinch cayenne pepper
- 1 (28 oz.) can crushed tomatoes
- 1 (15 oz.) can garbanzo beans, drained and rinsed
- 1 (8 oz.) can kidney beans, drained and rinsed
- 1/2 C. raisins
- salt and pepper to taste

Directions

1. In a large pan, heat the oil on medium heat and sauté the onion till tender.
2. Stir in the lentils, garlic, curry powder, cumin and cayenne pepper and cook for about 2 minutes.
3. Stir in the tomatoes, garbanzo beans, kidney beans, raisins, salt and pepper.
4. Reduce the heat to low and simmer for about 1 hour, stirring occasionally.

VIETNAMESE
Curry

Prep Time: 30 mins
Total Time: 2 hrs

Servings per Recipe: 8
Calories   479 kcal
Fat   26.5 g
Carbohydrates   51.4g
Protein   16.4 g
Cholesterol   0 mg
Sodium   271 mg

Ingredients

2 tbsp vegetable oil
1 onion, coarsely chopped
2 shallots, thinly sliced
2 cloves garlic, chopped
2 inch piece fresh ginger root, thinly sliced
1 stalk lemon grass, cut into 2 inch pieces
4 tbsp curry powder
1 green bell pepper, coarsely chopped
2 carrots, peeled and diagonally sliced
8 mushrooms, sliced
1 lb. fried tofu, cut into bite-size pieces
4 C. vegetable broth
4 C. water
2 tbsp vegetarian fish sauce
2 tsp red pepper flakes
1 bay leaf
2 kaffir lime leaves
8 small potatoes, quartered
1 (14 oz.) can coconut milk
2 C. fresh bean sprouts, for garnish
8 sprigs fresh chopped cilantro, for garnish

Directions

1. In a large pan, heat the oil on medium heat and sauté the onion and shallots till tender.
2. Stir in the garlic, ginger, lemon grass and curry powder and cook for about 5 minutes.
3. Stir in the green pepper, carrots, mushrooms, tofu, vegetable stock, water, fish sauce and red pepper flakes and bring to a boil.
4. Stir in the potatoes and coconut milk and bring to a boil.
5. Reduce the heat and simmer for about 40-60 minutes.
6. Serve with a garnishing of the bean sprouts and cilantro.

Crock Pot Curry

Prep Time: 20 mins
Total Time: 4 hr 20 mins

Servings per Recipe: 8
Calories   208 kcal
Fat   4.7 g
Carbohydrates   35.9 g
Protein   8.7 g
Cholesterol   0 mg
Sodium   298 mg

Ingredients

- 5 russet potatoes, peeled and cut into 1-inch cubes
- 1/4 C. curry powder
- 2 tbsp flour
- 1 tbsp chili powder
- 1/2 tsp red pepper flakes
- 1/2 tsp cayenne pepper
- 1 large green bell pepper, cut into strips
- 1 large red bell pepper, cut into strips
- 1 (1 oz.) package dry onion soup mix (such as Lipton(R))
- 1 (14 oz.) can unsweetened coconut cream
- water, as needed
- 1 1/2 C. matchstick-cut carrots
- 1 C. green peas
- 1/4 C. chopped fresh cilantro

Directions

1. In a small bowl, mix together the curry powder, flour, chili powder, red pepper flakes and cayenne pepper.
2. In the bottom of a slow cooker, place the potatoes and top with the curry powder mixture.
3. Add the red bell pepper, green bell pepper, onion soup mix and coconut cream and stir to combine.
4. Set the slow cooker on Low and cook, covered for about 3-4 hours.
5. Stir in the carrots and cook for about 30 minutes.
6. Stir in the peas and cook for about 30 minutes.
7. Serve with a garnishing of the cilantro.

AMERICAN
Yukon Curry

🥣 Prep Time: 20 mins
🕐 Total Time: 1 hr 5 mins

Servings per Recipe: 6
Calories   203 kcal
Fat   8.9 g
Carbohydrates   29.3g
Protein   4.1 g
Cholesterol   0 mg
Sodium   485 mg

Ingredients

1 head cabbage, cored and shredded
2 bunches green onions, chopped
1 (16 oz.) package frozen green peas
1 C. dry roasted peanuts
1 C. sour cream
1 C. mayonnaise

1/4 C. white vinegar
2 tbsp curry powder
1/2 tsp ground ginger
1 tsp ground cayenne pepper

Directions

1. In a Dutch oven, mix together the oil, curry powder and cumin on medium heat and cook till aromatic.
2. Stir in the eggplant, jalapeño peppers, potatoes, tomatoes, salt, chili powder and turmeric and cook, covered for about 30-45 minutes.
3. Serve with a sprinkling of the cilantro.

Asian Curried Coleslaw

Prep Time: 20 mins
Total Time: 20 mins

Servings per Recipe: 12
Calories   313 kcal
Fat   25.1 g
Carbohydrates   18.3g
Protein   7.7 g
Cholesterol   15 mg
Sodium   279 mg

Ingredients

- 1 head cabbage, cored and shredded
- 2 bunches green onions, chopped
- 1 (16 oz.) package frozen green peas
- 1 C. dry roasted peanuts
- 1 C. sour cream
- 1 C. mayonnaise
- 1/4 C. white vinegar
- 2 tbsp curry powder
- 1/2 tsp ground ginger
- 1 tsp ground cayenne pepper

Directions

1. In a large bowl, mix together the cabbage, green onions, peas, and peanuts.
2. In another bowl, add the sour cream, mayonnaise, vinegar, curry powder, ginger and cayenne pepper and beat till well combined.
3. Place the dressing over the salad and toss to coat well.

HYDERABADI
Curry

🍲 Prep Time: 10 mins
🕒 Total Time: 35 mins

Servings per Recipe: 4
Calories   371 kcal
Fat   19.2 g
Carbohydrates   46.6g
Protein   7.6 g
Cholesterol   31 mg
Sodium   256 mg

Ingredients
1/4 C. butter
2 tbsp olive oil
1/2 large onion, finely chopped
2 large carrots, sliced
2 tbsp curry powder
1/2 tsp ground turmeric

salt and ground black pepper to taste
1 pinch red pepper flakes
1 head cauliflower, broken into small florets
2 large potatoes, peeled and cubed

Directions
1. In a large skillet, heat the oil and butter on medium heat and cook the onion and carrots till tender.
2. Stir in the curry powder, turmeric, salt, pepper and red pepper flakes.
3. Add the cauliflower and potatoes and stir to combine well.
4. Reduce heat to medium-low and simmer, covered for about 20 minutes, stirring occasionally.

Madras Veggie Curry

Prep Time: 15 mins
Total Time: 1 hr

Servings per Recipe: 12
Calories	396 kcal
Fat	11.3 g
Carbohydrates	64.7g
Protein	11.3 g
Cholesterol	28 mg
Sodium	677 mg

Ingredients

- 3 tbsp ghee
- 1 tsp cumin seeds
- 1 tsp turmeric
- 1 tsp ground coriander
- 1 tsp salt
- 1/2 tsp mustard seed
- 1/2 tsp ground cayenne pepper
- 6 medium potatoes, peeled and diced
- 2 C. water
- 1 C. yogurt
- 2/3 C. frozen green peas

Directions

1. In a skillet, melt the ghee on medium heat and stir in the cumin, turmeric, coriander, salt, mustard seed and cayenne pepper.
2. Stir in the potatoes and cook for about 10 minutes, stirring occasionally.
3. Stir in the water.
4. Reduce the heat to low and simmer for about 30 minutes.
5. Stir in the yogurt and peas and cook till heated completely.

RESTAURANT STYLE
Okra

Prep Time: 5 mins
Total Time: 15 mins

Servings per Recipe: 4
Calories   69 kcal
Fat   3.7 g
Carbohydrates   8.5g
Protein   2.4 g
Cholesterol   0 mg
Sodium   301 mg

Ingredients
1 lb. okra, ends trimmed, cut into 1/4-inch rounds
1 tbsp olive oil
1 tsp whole cumin seeds
1/2 tsp curry powder
1/2 tsp chickpea flour
1/2 tsp salt

Directions
1. In a microwave safe bowl, add the okra and microwave on High for about 3 minutes.
2. In a large skillet, heat the olive oil on medium heat and sauté the cumin till it becomes golden brown.
3. Stir in the okra and cook for about 5 minutes.
4. Gently, stir in the curry powder, chickpea flour and salt and cook for about 2 minutes.
5. Serve immediately.

Microwave Okra Curry

Prep Time: 10 mins
Total Time: 25 mins

Servings per Recipe: 4
Calories	235.9
Fat	10 g
Cholesterol	0 mg
Sodium	665.8 mg
Carbohydrates	30.3 g
Protein	8.7 g

Ingredients

- 1 onion, sliced
- 2 tbsp green curry paste
- 3 C. okra, sliced
- 1 (400 g) can chickpeas, drained
- 1 C. light coconut milk
- 1 tbsp lemon juice
- 1 tbsp soy sauce
- 1/2 C. nuts, chopped

Directions

1. In a large microwave safe casserole dish, place the onion and curry paste and cook on Very High for about 2 minutes.
2. Add the okra, chick peas, coconut milk, lemon juice and soy sauce and cook on Very High for about 6-8 minutes.
3. Serve over the jasmine rice with a garnishing of the nuts.

SIMPLY
Lentils Curry

🥣 Prep Time: 20 mins
⏲ Total Time: 40 mins

Servings per Recipe: 2
Calories   145 kcal
Fat   0.5 g
Carbohydrates   25.2g
Protein   10.8 g
Cholesterol   0 mg
Sodium   146 mg

Ingredients
1/2 C. dried lentils
1 C. water
3/4 C. canned cream of coconut
1 tbsp curry paste
salt to taste

Directions
1. Rinse the lentils completely.
2. In a pan, add the lentils and water and bring to a boil.
3. Reduce the heat to low and simmer, covered for about 15 minutes.
4. Stir in the curry paste, coconut cream and salt and bring to a gentle boil.
5. Simmer for about 10-15 minutes.

Aunties' Chickpea Dinner

Prep Time: 10 mins
Total Time: 40 mins

Servings per Recipe: 8
Calories	135 kcal
Fat	4.5 g
Carbohydrates	20.5g
Protein	4.1 g
Cholesterol	0 mg
Sodium	289 mg

Ingredients

- 2 tbsp vegetable oil
- 2 onions, minced
- 2 cloves garlic, minced
- 2 tsp fresh ginger root, finely chopped
- 6 whole cloves
- 2 (2 inch) sticks cinnamon, crushed
- 1 tsp ground cumin
- 1 tsp ground coriander
- salt
- 1 tsp cayenne pepper
- 1 tsp ground turmeric
- 2 (15 oz.) cans garbanzo beans
- 1 C. chopped fresh cilantro

Directions

1. In a large frying pan, heat the oil on medium heat and sauté the onions till tender.
2. Stir in the garlic, ginger, cloves, cinnamon, cumin, coriander, salt, cayenne and turmeric and sauté for about 1 minute.
3. Stir in the garbanzo beans with the liquid and cook till heated completely.
4. Stir in the cilantro, reserving 1 tbsp and remove from the heat.
5. Serve with a garnishing of the reserved cilantro.

AMERICAN
Curry Corn

Prep Time: 10 mins
Total Time: 20 mins

Servings per Recipe: 4
Calories	214 kcal
Fat	15.3 g
Carbohydrates	19.1g
Protein	3.6 g
Cholesterol	36 mg
Sodium	80 mg

Ingredients
3 tbsp butter
2 C. frozen corn
2 tbsp chopped green bell pepper
2 tbsp chopped onion
1/2 tsp curry powder
1/2 C. sour cream
salt and ground black pepper to taste

Directions
1. In a large skillet, melt the butter on medium heat and cook the corn, green pepper, onion and curry powder, covered for about 8-10 minutes.
2. Stir in the sour cream, salt and pepper, and cook for about 2-3 minutes, stirring continuously.
3. Serve immediately.

Caterer's Curry Soup

Prep Time: 25 mins
Total Time: 1 hr 25 mins

Servings per Recipe: 8
Calories	108 kcal
Fat	0.8 g
Carbohydrates	24g
Protein	4.2 g
Cholesterol	0 mg
Sodium	196 mg

Ingredients
- 1 1/2 gallons vegetable broth
- 4 butternut squashes - peeled, seeded, and diced
- 6 bunches mustard greens, chopped
- 7 heads cauliflower, cut into florets
- 7 heads broccoli, cut into florets
- 7 red bell peppers, diced
- 15 carrots, peeled and diced
- 15 parsnips, diced
- 1 1/2 onions, diced
- 1 1/2 stalks celery, diced
- 3/4 C. raisins
- 1/4 C. curry powder
- 1/4 C. ground ginger
- 1/4 C. ground cumin
- 1 1/2 tsp cayenne pepper

Directions
1. In a large pan, add all the ingredients and bring to a boil.
2. Reduce the heat to medium-low and simmer for about 1 hour.

SUMMER Potluck Curry Salad

Prep Time: 20 mins
Total Time: 1 hr 20 mins

Servings per Recipe: 6
Calories 331 kcal
Fat 28.6 g
Carbohydrates 18.8g
Protein 3.8 g
Cholesterol 10 mg
Sodium 178 mg

Ingredients
1 large head broccoli, cut into florets
1/2 red bell pepper, chopped
1/2 C. dried cranberries
1/2 C. chopped walnuts
4 scallions, chopped
3/4 C. mayonnaise
2 tbsp fresh lime juice
2 tbsp apple cider vinegar
1 tbsp white sugar
1 tbsp curry powder, or more to taste
1/2 tsp cayenne pepper

Directions
1. In a large bowl, mix together the broccoli, red bell pepper, cranberries, walnuts and scallions.
2. In another bowl, add the mayonnaise, lime juice, vinegar, sugar, curry powder and cayenne pepper and beat till smooth.
3. Place the dressing mixture over the broccoli mixture and toss to coat well.
4. Refrigerate for about 2 hours to overnight.
5. Toss well and serve immediately.

Seema's Delight

Prep Time: 30 mins
Total Time: 1 hr 10 mins

Servings per Recipe: 6
Calories   312 kcal
Fat   3.8 g
Carbohydrates   63.5g
Protein   7.4 g
Cholesterol   4 mg
Sodium   280 mg

Ingredients

- 1 small onion, chopped
- 5 medium carrots, peeled and chopped
- 2 tsp butter
- 2 tsp olive oil
- 2 cloves garlic, minced
- 1 (28 oz.) can diced tomatoes
- 2 C. water
- 1 medium yam, peeled and diced
- 7 small red potatoes, cubed
- 2 C. cauliflower florets
- 1/2 tsp turmeric powder
- 2 tsp curry powder
- 1 tsp ground cumin
- 1/4 tsp garam masala
- 1/8 tsp cayenne pepper
- 1 tsp red pepper flakes

Directions

1. In a food processor, add the onion and carrots and pulse till minced very finely.
2. In a large pan, heat the oil and butter on medium heat and sauté the garlic till browned slightly.
3. Add the carrot mixture and bring to a gentle simmer.
4. Cook for about 5 minutes.
5. Add the diced tomatoes, water, yam, red potatoes, cauliflower, turmeric, curry powder, cumin, garam masala, cayenne and red pepper flakes and simmer for about 30 minutes.

VEGETARIAN
Chicken Curry

Prep Time: 15 mins
Total Time: 50 mins

Servings per Recipe: 4
Calories	273 kcal
Fat	10.3 g
Carbohydrates	30.7g
Protein	16.8 g
Cholesterol	0 mg
Sodium	1471 mg

Ingredients

- 2 tbsp vegetable oil
- 1 (12 oz.) package Quorn(TM) Chicken-Style Recipe Tenders, or vegetarian chicken alternative
- 1 medium onion, chopped
- 3 cloves garlic, crushed
- 1/2 tsp cumin seed
- 1/2 tsp black mustard seed
- 1 tsp ground turmeric
- 1 tsp ground cumin
- 1 tsp ground coriander
- 1 tsp chili powder
- 1 tsp salt
- 2 tsp tomato puree
- 1 (8 oz.) can chickpeas, drained
- 1 (14 oz.) can diced tomatoes
- 1 C. vegetable broth
- 1 tsp garam masala

Directions

1. In a large skillet, heat 1 tbsp of the oil on medium-high heat and cook the Quorn till golden brown.
2. Transfer the Quorn into a bowl and keep aside.
3. In the same pan, heat the remaining 1 tbsp of the oil on medium heat and sauté the onion, garlic, cumin seed and mustard seed for about 3-5 minutes.
4. Add the ground turmeric, cumin, and coriander, chili powder, salt, tomato puree and stir to combine well.
5. Stir in the Quorn, chickpeas, diced tomatoes and vegetable stock and bring to a boil.
6. Reduce the heat to medium-low and simmer for about 20-25 minutes.
7. Remove from the heat and stir in the garam masala.
8. Serve hot.

Quinoa Masala

Prep Time: 20 mins
Total Time: 1 hr 20 mins

Servings per Recipe: 4
Calories   413 kcal
Fat   10.5 g
Carbohydrates   62.1g
Protein   19.8 g
Cholesterol   9 mg
Sodium   1158 mg

Ingredients

- 1 tbsp olive oil
- 1 C. diced onion
- 1 C. chopped mushrooms
- 1/2 C. chopped carrots
- 3 cloves garlic, minced
- 4 C. vegetable broth
- 1 C. water
- 1 C. dry green lentils
- 1/2 C. quinoa
- 2 tbsp tomato paste
- 2 tbsp curry powder
- 1 tbsp ground red chili pepper
- 1 tbsp ground cumin
- 1 tbsp ground ginger
- 1 tsp cayenne pepper
- 1 tsp garam masala (Indian spice blend)
- 1 tsp ground turmeric
- 1 tsp salt, or to taste
- 1 dash ground black pepper
- 1/4 C. milk
- 1 tbsp butter

Directions

1. In a large pan, heat the oil on medium heat and sauté the onion for about 3 minutes.
2. Stir in the mushrooms, carrots and garlic and cook for about 2 minutes.
3. Stir in the vegetable broth, water, lentils, quinoa, tomato paste, curry powder, chili powder, cumin, ginger, cayenne pepper, garam masala, turmeric, salt and pepper.
4. Reduce the heat to medium-low and simmer, covered for about 40 minutes.
5. Stir in the butter and cream and simmer, covered for about 5 minutes.

MICROWAVE
Pea Curry

🍲 Prep Time: 10 mins
🕐 Total Time: 25 mins

Servings per Recipe: 4
Calories   235.9
Fat   10 g
Cholesterol   0 mg
Sodium   665.8 mg
Carbohydrates   30.3 g
Protein   8.7 g

Ingredients

1 onion, sliced
2 tbsp green curry paste
3 C. peas, sliced
1 (400 g) can chickpeas, drained
1 C. light coconut milk
1 tbsp lemon juice
1 tbsp soy sauce
1/2 C. nuts, chopped

Directions

1. In a large microwave safe casserole dish, place the onion and curry paste and cook on Very High for about 2 minutes.
2. Add the peas, chick peas, coconut milk, lemon juice and soy sauce and cook on Very High for about 6-8 minutes.
3. Serve over the jasmine rice with a garnishing of the nuts.

Spicy Squash Curry

Prep Time: 15 mins
Total Time: 1 hr

Servings per Recipe: 4
Calories   401 kcal
Fat   14 g
Carbohydrates   63.5g
Protein   10.1 g
Cholesterol   17 mg
Sodium   501 mg

Ingredients

- 2 acorn squash, halved and seeded
- 1 tbsp olive oil
- 1/2 C. diced red bell pepper
- 1/2 C. sliced daikon radish
- 1/4 C. sliced leek
- 1/4 C. diced celery
- 1 jalapeno pepper, diced
- 1 tbsp minced garlic
- 2 C. vegetable stock
- 1 C. brown rice
- 1 C. chopped collard greens
- 1 tbsp curry powder
- 1 1/2 tsp red curry paste
- 1/4 C. chopped walnuts
- 1/2 C. crumbled feta cheese

Directions

1. With the plastic wraps, wrap each squash half.
2. In the microwave, place the wrapped squash, cut side down and cook on High for about 12-15 minutes.
3. Remove from the microwave and keep aside, wrapped while preparing filling.
4. In a large skillet, heat the olive oil on medium heat and cook the red bell pepper, radish, leek, celery, jalapeño pepper and garlic for about 10 minutes.
5. Stir in the vegetable stock and rice and simmer, covered for about 45 minutes.
6. Uncover and stir in the collard greens.
7. Simmer, covered for about 5 minutes.
8. Stir in the curry powder, curry paste and walnuts and remove from the heat.
9. Unwrap the squash halves and place into 4 soup bowls, cut sides up.
10. Place about 2 tbsp of the feta cheese into each squash half and top with the rice mixture evenly.
11. Serve with a topping of the any leftover feta.

FULL
Indian Curry

🥣 Prep Time: 30 mins
🕐 Total Time: 55 mins

Servings per Recipe: 4
Calories   175 kcal
Fat   5.1 g
Carbohydrates   25.9 g
Protein   8.2 g
Cholesterol   0 mg
Sodium   178 mg

Ingredients
2 C. water
1/2 C. sliced cabbage
1/2 C. sliced carrot
1/2 C. fresh green beans, trimmed
1/2 C. sliced green bell pepper
1/2 C. yellow split peas
1 tbsp ground coriander
2 tsp sambar powder
1/2 tsp chili powder
1/2 tsp water
1 tbsp vegetable oil

1 tsp cumin seeds
1/2 tsp mustard seed
1 pinch asafoetida powder
1/2 tsp ground turmeric
2 tbsp chopped fresh cilantro
2 tbsp fresh grated coconut
2 tsp tamarind pulp
1 tsp brown sugar
salt to taste

Directions
1. In a pressure cooker, add 2 C. of the water, cabbage, carrot, green beans, bell pepper and yellow split peas.
2. Secure the lid and place pressure regulator over vent pipe.
3. Bring to a high pressure and cook for about 6-8 minutes.
4. Use the quick release method to release the pressure.
5. Drain the mixture and reserve the excess liquid.
6. Reserve the vegetable mixture into a bowl.
7. In a small bowl, add the ground coriander, sambar powder, chili powder, and 1/2 tsp of the water and mix till a paste forms.
8. In a skillet, heat the vegetable oil on medium-high heat and sauté the cumin seeds and mustard seeds for about 1 minute.
9. Stir in the asafoetida powder and sambar paste and sauté for about 1 minute.
10. Stir in the turmeric and the reserved vegetable mixture. (Add the reserved cooking liquid

if vegetable mixture is too thick.)
11. Stir in the cilantro, coconut, tamarind pulp, brown sugar and salt and simmer for about 10-15 minutes.

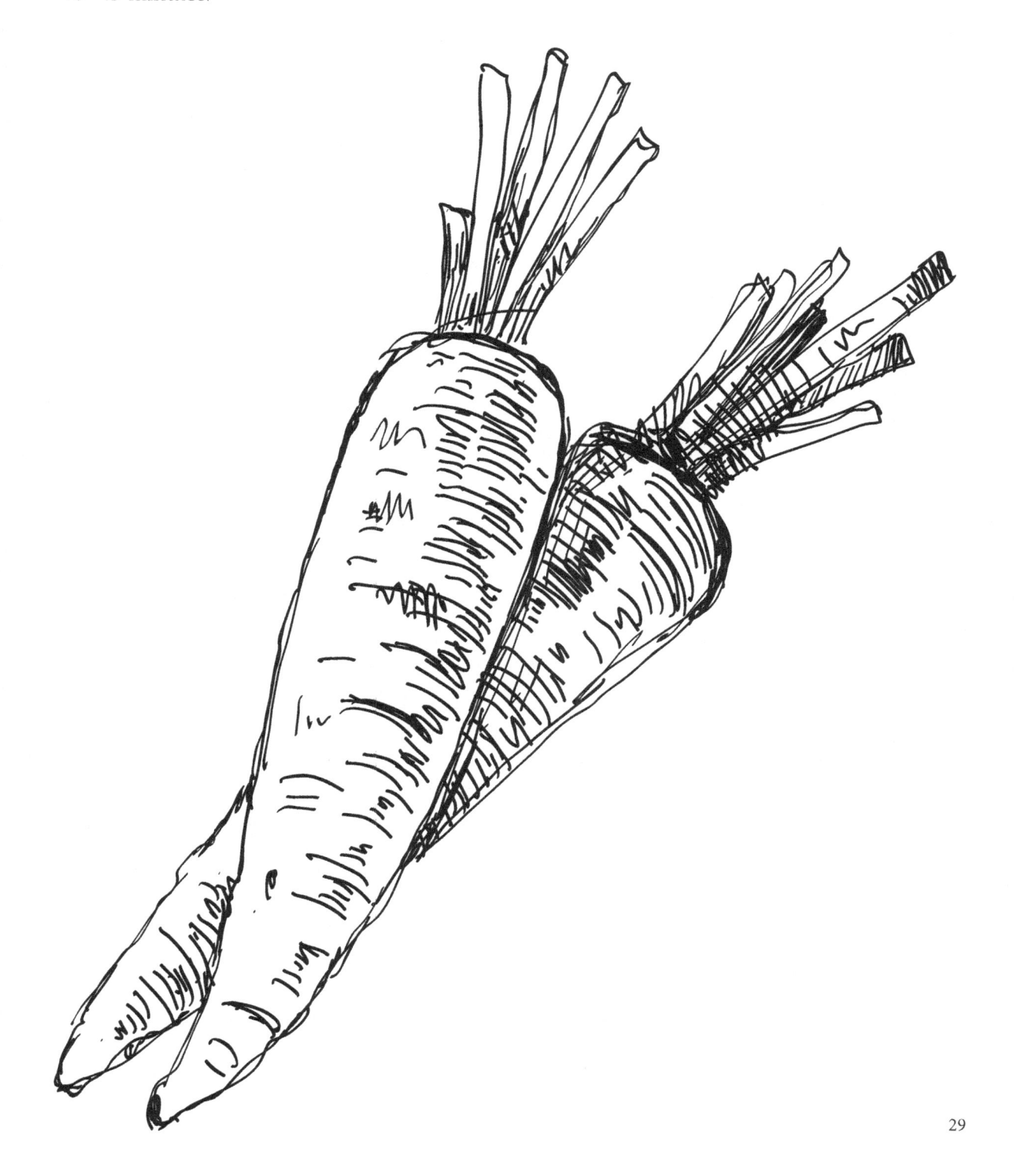

CURRIED
Rice Salad

Prep Time: 30 mins
Total Time: 55 mins

Servings per Recipe: 8
Calories   168 kcal
Fat   6.9 g
Carbohydrates   19.2g
Protein   9.6 g
Cholesterol   2 mg
Sodium   325 mg

Ingredients

1/2 C. white rice
2 C. extra-firm tofu, drained and cubed
1 C. yogurt
2 tbsp lime juice
1 tbsp curry powder
1 C. halved grapes
1 tbsp dried cranberries
1/2 C. diced celery
3 tbsp diced green onions

1/4 C. walnuts
salt and pepper to taste

Directions

1. In a pan of the boiling water, stir in the rice.
2. Reduce the heat and simmer for about 20 minutes.
3. Remove from the heat and keep aside.
4. In another large pan of the boiling water, cook the cubed tofu for about 3 minutes.
5. Drain well and keep aside to cool.
6. In a bowl, mix together the yogurt, lime juice and curry powder.
7. In a large bowl, mix together the halved grapes, cranberries, celery, green onions, walnuts, rice and tofu.
8. Place with the curry dressing, salt and pepper and toss to coat well.

Authentic Jamaican Curry

🥣 Prep Time: 20 mins
🕐 Total Time: 50 mins

Servings per Recipe: 6
Calories   190 kcal
Fat   9.4 g
Carbohydrates   25.8g
Protein   2.7 g
Cholesterol   0 mg
Sodium   19 mg

Ingredients

1 tsp ground cumin
1/2 tsp ground turmeric
1/2 tsp curry powder
1/2 tsp ground allspice
1/4 C. olive oil
1 tbsp grated fresh ginger root
1 small onion, chopped
4 cloves garlic, minced
2 potatoes, cut into small cubes
1/2 C. chopped red bell pepper
1/2 C. chopped broccoli
1 C. chopped bok choy
1 plantains, peeled and broken into chunks
1 C. water
salt to taste

Directions

1. In a bowl, mix together the cumin, turmeric, allspice and curry powder.
2. In a skillet, heat the olive oil on medium-low heat and sauté the ginger and cumin mixture for about 5 minutes.
3. Stir in the onion and garlic and sauté for about 1-2 minutes.
4. Stir in the potatoes and cook for about 1-2 minutes.
5. Stir in the red bell pepper, broccoli, bok choy, plantains and enough water to reach about half-full and cook, covered for about 20-25 minutes.
6. Stir in the salt and serve.

NORTH INDIAN Curried Cauliflower

Prep Time: 5 mins
Total Time: 15 mins

Servings per Recipe: 4
Calories   95 kcal
Fat   4.1 g
Carbohydrates   12.9 g
Protein   4.4 g
Cholesterol   2 mg
Sodium   56 mg

Ingredients

2 tbsp unsweetened coconut cream
5 tbsp milk
1 tbsp tamarind pulp
2 tbsp boiling water
1 tbsp chickpea flour
1/2 tsp chili powder
1 tsp coriander seed
1 head cauliflower, broken into small florets

1 tsp mustard seed
2 tbsp vegetable oil for frying
salt to taste

Directions

1. In a bowl, dissolve the coconut cream in 5 tbsp of the milk.
2. In another bowl, soak the tamarind in 2 tbsp of the boiling water for about 5-10 minutes.
3. Squeeze the husk and discard the tamarind piece, reserving the water.
4. In a bowl, add the tamarind water, flour, chili powder and coriander and mix till well combined.
5. Add the cauliflower and coconut milk and stir to coat well.
6. In a pan, heat the oil and sauté the mustard seeds till they start to pop.
7. Add the cauliflower mixture and simmer, covered till the cauliflower becomes tender, stirring occasionally.

Rustic Thai Mushroom Curry

Prep Time: 10 mins
Total Time: 30 mins

Servings per Recipe: 4
Calories   261 kcal
Fat   24.4 g
Carbohydrates   11.8 g
Protein   4.9 g
Cholesterol   0 mg
Sodium   1458 mg

Ingredients

- 2 C. coconut milk
- 1 (2 inch) piece galangal, peeled and sliced
- 3 kaffir lime leaves, torn
- 2 tsp salt
- 1/3 lb. sliced fresh mushrooms
- 5 Thai chili peppers, chopped
- 1/4 C. fresh lime juice
- 1 tbsp fish sauce

Directions

1. In a pan, add the coconut milk and galangal and bring to a boil.
2. Add the kaffir lime leaves and salt and simmer for about 10 minutes.
3. Add the mushrooms and cook for about 5-7 minutes.
4. Remove from the heat and stir in the lime juice and fish sauce.
5. Serve with a topping of the Thai chilies.

MICROWAVE
Broccoli Curry

Prep Time: 5 mins
Total Time: 25 mins

Servings per Recipe: 4
Calories 235.9
Fat 10 g
Cholesterol 0 mg
Sodium 665.8 mg
Carbohydrates 30.3 g
Protein 8.7 g

Ingredients
1 onion, sliced
2 tbsp red curry paste
3 C. broccoli, sliced
1 (400 g) can chickpeas, drained
1 C. light coconut milk
1 tbsp lemon juice
1 tbsp soy sauce
1/2 C. nuts, chopped

Directions
1. In a large microwave safe casserole dish, place the onion and curry paste and cook on Very High for about 2 minutes.
2. Add the broccoli, chick peas, coconut milk, lemon juice and soy sauce and cook on Very High for about 6-8 minutes.
3. Serve over the jasmine rice with a garnishing of the nuts.

Saturday Night Curry

Prep Time: 25 mins
Total Time: 40 mins

Servings per Recipe: 6
Calories   232 kcal
Fat   13.2 g
Carbohydrates   16.9 g
Protein   16.5 g
Cholesterol   0 mg
Sodium   680 mg

Ingredients

- 2 bunches green onions
- 1 (14 oz.) can light coconut milk
- 1/4 C. soy sauce, divided
- 1/2 tsp brown sugar
- 1 1/2 tsp curry powder
- 1 tsp minced fresh ginger
- 2 tsp chili paste
- 1 lb. firm tofu, cut into 3/4 inch cubes
- 4 roma (plum) tomatoes, chopped
- 1 yellow bell pepper, thinly sliced
- 4 oz. fresh mushrooms, chopped
- 1/4 C. chopped fresh basil
- 4 C. chopped bok choy
- salt to taste

Directions

1. Chop the white parts of the green onions finely.
2. Chop the green parts of the green onions into 2-inch pieces.
3. In a large heavy skillet, mix together the coconut milk, 3 tbsp of the soy sauce, brown sugar, curry powder, ginger and chili paste and bring to a boil.
4. Stir in the tofu, tomatoes, yellow pepper, mushrooms and white part of the green onions and cook, covered for about 5 minutes, stirring occasionally.
5. Stir in the basil, bok choy, salt and remaining soy sauce and cook for about 5 minutes.
6. Serve with a garnishing of the green parts of the green onion.

OCTOBER'S Apple Curry

Prep Time: 30 mins
Total Time: 2 hr 10 mins

Servings per Recipe: 6
Calories 360 kcal
Fat 3.7 g
Carbohydrates 64.3g
Protein 20.1 g
Cholesterol 0 mg
Sodium 244 mg

Ingredients

1 C. red lentils
1 C. brown lentils
8 C. water
1/2 tsp turmeric
1 tbsp canola oil
1 large onion, diced
2 tomatoes, cored and chopped
3 cloves garlic, minced
1 1/2 tbsp curry powder
2 tsp ground cumin
1/2 tsp salt
1/2 tsp black pepper
1/4 tsp ground cloves
2 C. peeled, cubed (1-inch), seeded pumpkin
2 potatoes, unpeeled and chopped
2 carrots, peeled and diced
2 C. packed fresh spinach, chopped
1 Granny Smith apple, unpeeled, cored and diced

Directions

1. In a pan, add the both lentils, water and turmeric on medium-low heat and cook for about 45 minutes.
2. Drain well, reserving 2 1/2 C. of the cooking liquid.
3. Meanwhile in a large deep pan, heat the canola oil on medium heat and sauté the onion for about 5 minutes.
4. Stir in the tomatoes and garlic and cook for about 5 minutes, stirring occasionally.
5. Stir in the curry powder, cumin, salt, pepper and cloves.
6. Increase the heat to medium-low and stir in the cooked lentil, reserved cooking liquid, pumpkin, potatoes and carrots and simmer, covered for about 35-45 minutes.
7. Stir in the spinach and apple and simmer for about 15 minutes.

Lunch Box
Soup Curry

Prep Time: 15 mins
Total Time: 40 mins

Servings per Recipe: 6
Calories	133 kcal
Fat	5.4 g
Carbohydrates	20.2g
Protein	2.4 g
Cholesterol	0 mg
Sodium	415 mg

Ingredients
2 tbsp vegetable oil
1 onion, chopped
1 tbsp curry powder
2 lb. carrots, chopped
4 C. vegetable broth
2 C. water

Directions
1. In a large pan, heat the oil on medium heat and sauté the onion till tender.
2. Stir in the curry powder.
3. Add the chopped carrots and stir to combine well.
4. Add the vegetable broth and simmer for about 20 minutes.
5. Remove from the heat and keep aside to cool slightly.
6. Transfer the soup mixture into a blender and pulse till smooth.
7. Return the soup in the pan and, add enough water to thin according to your required consistency.
8. Cook till heated completely before serving.

WHOLE GRAIN
Curry

Prep Time: 10 mins
Total Time: 8 hr 40 mins

Servings per Recipe: 4
Calories   278 kcal
Fat   9.1 g
Carbohydrates   42.9g
Protein   6.4 g
Cholesterol   0 mg
Sodium   592 mg

Ingredients
1 C. millet
2 tbsp olive oil
1 onion, diced
2 cloves garlic, diced
2 1/2 C. water
1 tsp salt
1/2 tsp ground cumin
2 tsp curry powder

Directions
1. In a large bowl of the water, soak the millet for about 8 hours to overnight.
2. Drain the millet completely.
3. In a large skillet, heat the oil on medium heat and sauté the onion and garlic for about 10-15 minutes.
4. Stir in the millet, 2 1/2 C. of the water, salt and cumin and simmer, covered for about 20 minutes.
5. Stir in the curry powder and remove from the heat.

Vegetarian Curry Japanese Style

- Prep Time: 30 mins
- Total Time: 1 hr

Servings per Recipe: 2
Calories	297 kcal
Fat	11.6 g
Carbohydrates	45.1g
Protein	8 g
Cholesterol	0 mg
Sodium	236 mg

Ingredients

- 2 C. cubed Japanese turnips
- 1 potato, peeled and cubed
- 1 tomato, diced
- 1 C. water
- 1/4 tsp ground turmeric

Spice Paste:
- 1 tsp canola oil
- 2 dried red chilis
- 2 small Thai green chilis
- 1 (1/2 inch) piece cinnamon stick
- 4 pearl onions
- 2 tbsp unsweetened dried coconut
- 1 tbsp coriander seeds
- 5 cashews
- 2 green cardamom pods
- 2 whole cloves
- 1/2 tsp fennel seeds
- 1/4 tsp cumin seeds
- 2 tbsp chopped cilantro
- 2 tbsp chopped fresh mint
- 1 tsp water, or as needed
- 1 tsp canola oil
- 1/2 tsp fennel seeds
- 1 (1 inch) piece cinnamon stick
- 2 cloves garlic, minced
- 1 (1 inch) piece fresh ginger root, minced
- 4 fresh curry leaves
- 1/4 C. peas
- 1 pinch salt

Directions

1. In a large pan, add the turnips, potato, diced tomato, 1 C. of the water and turmeric and bring to a boil.
2. Reduce the heat and simmer for about 15 minutes.
3. In a skillet, heat 1 tsp of the canola oil on medium heat and sauté the chilis, 1/2-inch piece of the cinnamon stick, pearl onions, coconut, coriander, cashews, cardamom pods, cloves, 1/2 tsp of the fennel seeds and cumin seeds for about 3 minutes.
4. Remove from the heat and transfer into a spice grinder.
5. Add the cilantro, mint and 1 tsp of the water and grind till a smooth paste forms.

6. In a large skillet, heat 1 tsp of the canola oil on medium-low heat and sauté 1/2 tsp of the fennel seeds and 1-inch piece of the cinnamon stick for about 30 seconds.
7. Add the minced garlic, ginger and curry leaves and sauté for about 2 minutes.
8. Add the cooked vegetables and spice paste and bring to a boil. (Add more water if curry becomes too thick.)
9. Stir in the green peas and salt.
10. Reduce the heat and simmer for about 10 minutes.

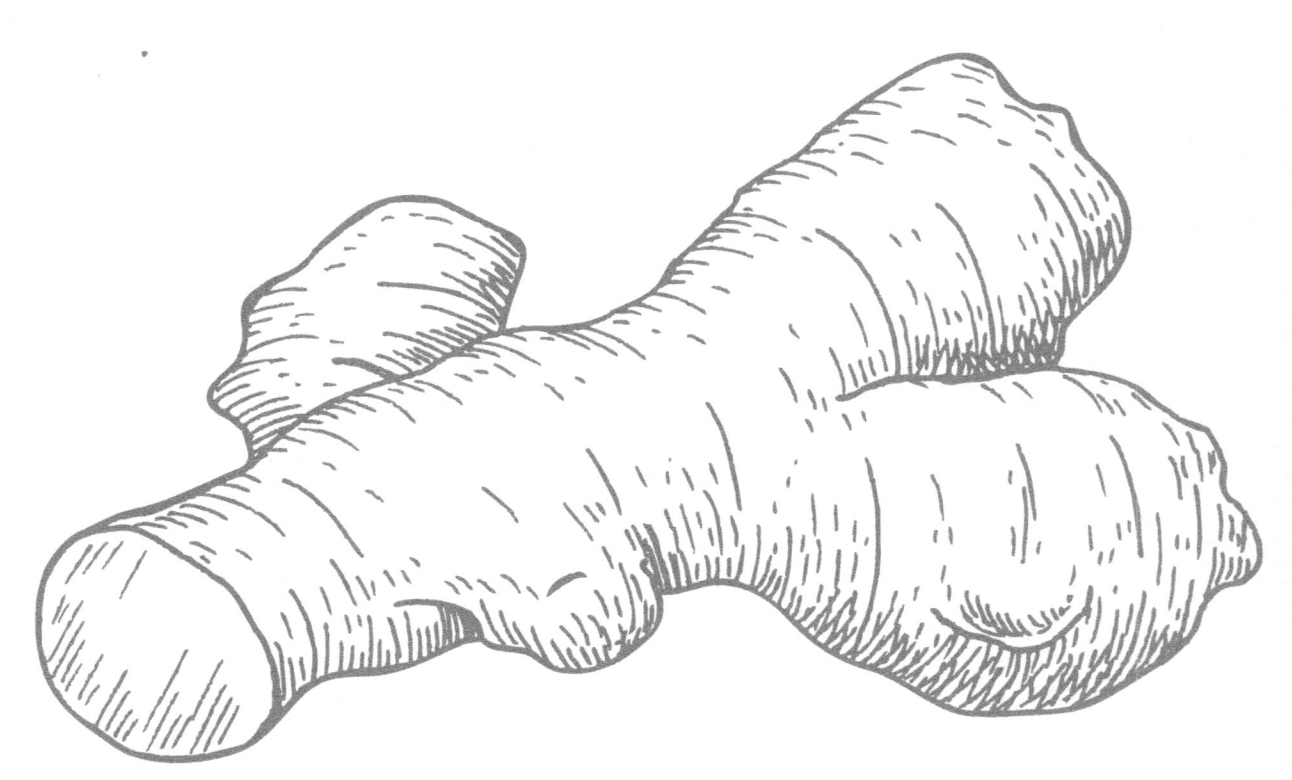

Curry Salad

Prep Time: 20 mins
Total Time: 20 mins

Servings per Recipe: 2
Calories   292 kcal
Fat   16.3 g
Carbohydrates   40.4 g
Protein   3 g
Cholesterol   0 mg
Sodium   127 mg

Ingredients

- 1 sweet apple, grated
- 2 carrots, grated
- 1/4 C. raisins
- 2 tbsp chopped fresh parsley

Dressing:
- 1 lemon, juiced
- 2 tbsp olive oil
- 1 tbsp toasted sesame seeds
- 1 tsp curry powder
- 1/2 tsp maple syrup
- salt and ground black pepper to taste

Directions

1. In a large bowl, mix together the apple, carrots, raisins and parsley.
2. In a container with a tight-fitting lid, mix together the remaining ingredients.
3. Cover the jar tightly and shake till well combined.
4. Place the dressing over the salad and mix till well combined.

SOUTH EAST ASIAN
All-Ingredient Curry

Prep Time: 20 mins
Total Time: 2 hr 20 mins

Servings per Recipe: 4
Calories 765 kcal
Fat 38.5 g
Carbohydrates 90.6g
Protein 20.6 g
Cholesterol 0 mg
Sodium 749 mg

Ingredients
Brown Rice:
3 C. water
2 C. brown rice
1 tbsp soy sauce
1/2 tsp salt
Panang Curry:
1 tbsp vegetable oil
2 1/2 tbsp red curry paste
1 (14 oz.) can coconut milk
1 tbsp vegetarian fish sauce

1 tbsp white sugar
5 kaffir lime leaves
8 oz. fried tofu, cubed
2 C. broccoli florets
1/2 red bell pepper, chopped into 1-inch pieces
1/4 C. diagonally sliced carrots

Directions
1. In a rice cooker, mix together the water, brown rice, soy sauce and salt.
2. Cook, covered about 35 minutes according to manufacturer's directions.
3. In a wide skillet, heat the vegetable oil on medium heat and sauté the curry paste for about 1-2 minutes.
4. Add the coconut milk, fish sauce, white sugar and lime leaves and stir to combine.
5. Reduce the heat to medium-low and simmer, covered for about 5 minutes.
6. Stir in the tofu, broccoli, red bell pepper and carrots and simmer for about 1-2 minutes.
7. Serve this curry over the cooked brown rice.

Punjabi Greens Curry

Prep Time: 15 mins
Total Time: 35 mins

Servings per Recipe: 2
Calories	333 kcal
Fat	20.1 g
Carbohydrates	22.7g
Protein	18.9 g
Cholesterol	17 mg
Sodium	7499 mg

Ingredients

- 2 tbsp vegetable oil, divided
- 2 C. chopped fresh spinach
- 1 tsp ground cumin
- 3/4 C. chopped onion
- 2 green chili peppers, chopped
- 2 tsp chopped garlic
- 2 tomatoes, chopped
- 1/2 C. water
- 2 tsp ground coriander
- 1 tsp ground red chilis
- 2 tbsp salt
- 8 oz. paneer, cubed

Directions

1. In a skillet, heat 1 tbsp of the vegetable oil on medium heat and cook the spinach for about 3-4 minutes.
2. Remove from the heat and keep aside to cool slightly.
3. Transfer the spinach into a food processor and pulse till a rough paste forms.
4. In a pan, heat the remaining 1 tbsp of the oil on medium heat and sauté the cumin for about 30 seconds.
5. Add the onion, green chili peppers and garlic and sauté for about 3-4 minutes.
6. Stir in the tomatoes and simmer, covered for about 1 minute.
7. Add the spinach paste, water, ground coriander, red chili powder and salt and cook for about 2-3 minutes.
8. Stir in the paneer and simmer for about 1-2 minutes more.

EASY VEGGIE Curry Soup from Vietnam

Prep Time: 20 mins
Total Time: 37 mins

Servings per Recipe: 4
Calories   264 kcal
Fat   22.1 g
Carbohydrates   16.4g
Protein   6.1 g
Cholesterol   6 mg
Sodium   1331 mg

Ingredients

1/2 onion, diced
2 1/2 tbsp curry powder
1 (32 fluid oz.) container chicken broth
1/2 lemon, sliced
1 1/4-inch-thick slices fresh ginger, peeled
1 1/2 tsp white sugar
salt to taste
1 lb. assorted mushrooms
1 (13.5 oz.) can coconut milk
1 tbsp fresh lemon juice
salt to taste
8 kaffir lime leaves

Directions

1. Heat a greased pan on high heat and sauté the onion for about 2 minutes.
2. Stir in the curry powder.
3. Add the chicken broth, lemon, ginger, sugar and salt and stir to combine.
4. Reduce the heat to medium and cook for about 2-3 minutes.
5. Stir in the mushrooms and cook for about 3 minutes.
6. Stir in in the coconut milk and lemon juice and remove from the heat.
7. Stir in the lime leaves and keep aside for about 5 minutes.
8. Discard the lime leaves before serving.

Vegetarian Curry Sri Lankan Style

Prep Time: 20 mins
Total Time: 35 mins

Servings per Recipe: 4
Calories   381 kcal
Fat   9.8 g
Carbohydrates   67.9 g
Protein   8.6 g
Cholesterol   8 mg
Sodium   609 mg

Ingredients

- 3/4 tsp coriander seed
- 1/4 tsp fennel seed
- 1/4 tsp cumin seed
- 4 leaves fresh curry
- 4 large potatoes - peeled and cubed
- 1 tbsp ghee (clarified butter)
- 1/2 onion, finely chopped
- 1 clove garlic, minced
- 1 (1 inch) piece fresh ginger root, grated
- 1/2 tsp cumin seed
- 1/2 tsp coriander seed
- 1/2 C. coconut milk
- 1 tbsp chopped fresh cilantro
- salt to taste

Directions

1. For the fresh curry powder, in a small skillet, dry roast the 3/4 tsp of the coriander, 1/4 tsp of the fennel, and 1/4 tsp of the cumin seeds individually till aromatic.
2. In the same skillet, mix together all the roasted spices and curry leaves on low heat and dry roast for about 5 minutes more.
3. With a mortar and pestle, grind the spices and curry leaves.
4. Now, with the mortar and pestle, grind the remaining coriander and cumin seeds.
5. In a microwave safe bowl, place the potato cubes and microwave for about 3-5 minutes.
6. In a large skillet, melt the ghee on medium heat and sauté the onion, garlic and ginger till golden and aromatic.
7. Add the cumin and coriander seeds powder and fresh curry powder and sauté for about 30 seconds.
8. Stir in the potatoes and cook for about 3 minutes.
9. Stir in the coconut milk and bring to a gentle boil.
10. Reduce the heat to low and simmer, covered for about 7 minutes.
11. Stir in the salt and remove from the heat.

12. Serve with a topping of the chopped fresh cilantro.

Peanut Thai Curry

Prep Time: 5 mins
Total Time: 30 mins

Servings per Recipe: 6
Calories 581 kcal
Fat 22.8 g
Carbohydrates 79.3g
Protein 16.4 g
Cholesterol 0 mg
Sodium 1078 mg

Ingredients
- 1 1/2 C. white rice
- 3 C. water
- 1 (14 oz.) can coconut milk
- 5 tbsp peanut butter
- 2 (14.5 oz.) cans chickpeas (garbanzo beans), rinsed and drained
- 2 tsp ground ginger
- 1/8 tsp ground cinnamon
- 1/8 tsp cayenne pepper
- 1 (28 oz.) can diced tomatoes, drained
- 1 tsp salt

Directions
1. In a pan, add the rice and water and bring to a boil.
2. Reduce the heat to medium-low and simmer, covered for about 20-25 minutes.
3. Meanwhile in another large pan, mix together the coconut milk and peanut butter on medium-high heat and cook for about 5-7 minutes.
4. Stir in the chickpeas, ginger, cinnamon and cayenne pepper and cook for about 10 minutes, stirring occasionally.
5. Add the tomatoes and cook for about 10 minutes.
6. Stir in the salt and remove from the heat.
7. Serve the curry over the rice.

TRADITIONAL
North Indian Beans Curry

🥣 Prep Time: 10 mins
🕐 Total Time: 1 hr 10 mins

Servings per Recipe: 8
Calories   224 kcal
Fat   5.5 g
Carbohydrates   34.2g
Protein   11.3 g
Cholesterol   3 mg
Sodium   16 mg

Ingredients

- 2 C. dry red kidney beans
- 1 large onion, chopped
- 4 cloves garlic, chopped
- 1 (2 inch) piece fresh ginger root, chopped
- 2 tbsp vegetable oil
- 2 tsp ghee (clarified butter)
- 2 dried red chili peppers, broken into pieces
- 1 tsp cumin seeds
- 6 whole cloves
- 1 tsp ground turmeric
- 1 tsp ground cumin
- 1 tsp ground coriander
- 2 tomatoes, chopped
- 2 C. water
- 1 tsp white sugar
- salt to taste
- 2 tsp garam masala
- 1 tsp ground red pepper
- 1/4 C. cilantro leaves, chopped

Directions

1. In a large bowl, of water, soak the kidney beans for about 8 hours or overnight.
2. Drain and rinse the kidney beans.
3. With a mortar and pestle, grind the onion, ginger and garlic till a paste forms.
4. In a pressure cooker, heat the oil and ghee on medium heat and sauté the red chili peppers, cumin seeds and whole cloves till the cumin seeds begin to splutter.
5. Stir in the onion paste and cook till golden brown, stirring occasionally.
6. Stir in the ground turmeric, ground cumin and ground coriander and sauté for a few seconds more.
7. Add the tomatoes and cook till the tomatoes become tender completely.
8. Add the drained kidney beans and enough water to cover.
9. Add extra 2 C. of the water, sugar and salt and stir to combine.
10. Secure the lid and place pressure regulator over vent pipe.
11. Bring to a high pressure and cook for about 40 minutes.
12. Reduce the heat to low and cook for about 10-15 minutes.

13. Use the natural release method to release the pressure.
14. Stir in the garam masala and ground red pepper and serve with a garnishing of the chopped cilantro.

VEGGIE CURRY
Burgers

Prep Time: 30 mins
Total Time: 50 mins

Servings per Recipe: 6
Calories	645 kcal
Fat	35.1 g
Carbohydrates	53.4g
Protein	34.2 g
Cholesterol	31 mg
Sodium	1235 mg

Ingredients
- 1 (15 oz.) can black beans, rinsed and drained
- 1 tbsp finely chopped red onion
- 1 clove garlic, minced
- 1/2 tsp salt
- 1 tsp Thai chili sauce
- 1 tsp red curry paste
- 2 tbsp coconut milk
- 1 tsp brown sugar
- 1 pinch cayenne pepper
- 1 egg
- 1 C. Italian bread crumbs
- 1 (1 lb.) package crumbled tofu
- 1 (12 oz.) package vegetarian burger crumbles
- 1 C. chunky peanut butter
- 1 tsp Thai chili sauce
- 1 tsp brown sugar
- 1/2 tsp salt
- 1/2 tsp ground turmeric
- 1 dash soy sauce
- 1 tbsp canola oil
- 6 whole wheat hamburger buns
- 1/2 C. shredded carrots
- 1/2 C. shredded cucumber
- 1 tbsp chopped green onion
- 2 tbsp fresh mint leaves
- 2 tbsp fresh cilantro leaves

Directions
1. In a food processor, add the black beans, red onion, garlic, 1/2 tsp of the salt, 1 tsp of the chili sauce, curry paste, coconut milk, 1 tsp of the brown sugar, cayenne pepper and egg and pulse till smooth.
2. Transfer the beans mixture into a large bowl.
3. Gently, fold in the bread crumbs and burger crumbles.
4. Make 6 equal sized patties from the mixture.
5. Arrange the patties onto a waxed paper lined tray and freeze for at least 30 minutes to set.
6. Heat a greased grill pan on medium heat and cook the patties for about 4-5 minutes per side.
7. Meanwhile in a pan, add the peanut butter, 1 tsp of the chili sauce, 1 tsp of the brown

sugar, 1/2 tsp of the salt, turmeric, soy sauce and canola oil on medium-low heat and cook till melted, stirring continuously.
8. Reduce the heat to low and simmer for about 3-5 minutes.
9. Arrange the patties over the bottom of each hamburger buns and drizzle with the sauce.
10. Top with the carrot, cucumber, green onion, mint and cilantro evenly and cover with the remaining bun halves.
11. Serve immediately.

POTATO CURRY
for Winter

Prep Time: 30 mins
Total Time: 1 hr

Servings per Recipe: 6
Calories   407 kcal
Fat   20.1 g
Carbohydrates   50.6 g
Protein   10.1 g
Cholesterol   0 mg
Sodium   1176 mg

Ingredients
4 potatoes, peeled and cubed
2 tbsp vegetable oil
1 yellow onion, diced
3 cloves garlic, minced
2 tsp ground cumin
1 1/2 tsp cayenne pepper
4 tsp curry powder
4 tsp garam masala
1 (1 inch) piece fresh ginger root, peeled and minced
2 tsp salt
1 (14.5 oz.) can diced tomatoes
1 (15 oz.) can garbanzo beans (chickpeas), rinsed and drained
1 (15 oz.) can peas, drained
1 (14 oz.) can coconut milk

Directions
1. In a large pan of salted water, add the potatoes on high heat and bring to a boil.
2. Reduce the heat to medium-low and simmer, covered for about 15 minutes.
3. Drain well and keep aside to steam dry for about 1-2 minutes.
4. Meanwhile in a large skillet, heat the vegetable oil on medium heat and sauté the onion and garlic for about 5 minutes.
5. Stir in the cumin, cayenne pepper, curry powder, garam masala, ginger and salt and sauté for about 2 minutes.
6. Add the tomatoes, garbanzo beans, peas, potatoes and coconut milk and bring to a gentle boil.
7. Simmer for about 5-10 minutes.
8. Serve hot.

Thai Tofu Curry

Prep Time: 20 mins
Total Time: 45 mins

Servings per Recipe: 4
Calories	536 kcal
Fat	37.9 g
Carbohydrates	44.2g
Protein	23.2 g
Cholesterol	0 mg
Sodium	312 mg

Ingredients

1 1/2 C. water
1 C. uncooked basmati rice, rinsed and drained
3 tbsp sesame oil
1 (14 oz.) package firm water-packed tofu, drained and cubed
1/4 tsp salt
1 (10 oz.) can coconut milk
2 tbsp green curry paste

Directions

1. In a medium pan, add the water and rice and bring to a boil.
2. Reduce the heat and simmer, covered for about 20 minutes.
3. Remove from heat and keep aside to cool slightly.
4. With a fork, fluff the rice.
5. In another medium pan, heat the sesame oil on medium heat and cook the tofu for about 20 minutes, stirring occasionally.
6. Stir in the salt and remove from the heat.
7. In a small pan, add the coconut milk and bring to a boil.
8. Add the green curry paste and stir to combine.
9. Reduce the heat and simmer for about 5 minutes.
10. Divide the rice and tofu into the serving plates and serve with a topping of the curry sauce.

WESTERN
Moroccan Curry

🥣 Prep Time: 15 mins
🕐 Total Time: 50 mins

Servings per Recipe: 6
Calories   330 kcal
Fat   18 g
Carbohydrates   39 g
Protein   8 g
Cholesterol   0 mg
Sodium   874 mg

Ingredients

1 sweet potato, peeled and cubed
1 medium eggplant, cubed
1 green bell pepper, chopped
1 red bell pepper, chopped
2 carrots, chopped
1 onion, chopped
6 tbsp olive oil
3 cloves garlic, minced
1 tsp ground turmeric
1 tbsp curry powder
1 tsp ground cinnamon

3/4 tbsp sea salt
3/4 tsp cayenne pepper
1 (15 oz.) can garbanzo beans, drained
1/4 C. blanched almonds
1 zucchini, sliced
2 tbsp raisins
1 C. orange juice
10 oz. spinach

Directions

1. In a large Dutch oven, heat 3 tbsp of the oil on medium heat and sauté the sweet potato, eggplant, peppers, carrots and onion for about 5 minutes.
2. Meanwhile in a medium pan, heat the remaining olive oil on medium heat and sauté the garlic, turmeric, curry powder, cinnamon, salt and pepper for about 3 minutes.
3. Add the garlic mixture in the Dutch oven and stir to combine.
4. Add the garbanzo beans, almonds, zucchini, raisins and orange juice and simmer, covered for about 20 minutes.
5. Stir in the spinach and simmer for about 5 minutes.
6. Serve hot.

Squash, Eggplant and Tomato Curry from Brazil

Prep Time: 45 mins
Total Time: 1 hr

Servings per Recipe: 6
Calories   432.8
Fat   14.9 g
Cholesterol   0 mg
Sodium   230.9 mg
Carbohydrates   72.8 g
Protein   8 g

Ingredients

- 1 butternut squash, peeled and 2 cm dice
- 2 red onions, roughly chopped
- 1 aubergine, chopped
- 2 red peppers, diced
- 1 (400 g) can chickpeas
- 2 garlic cloves, crushed
- 1/2 inch gingerroot, chopped
- 1 red chili pepper, deseeded and chopped
- 400 g chopped tomatoes
- 200 ml coconut cream
- 4 tbsp chopped fresh coriander
- 3 tbsp olive oil

Directions

1. Set your oven to 390 degrees F before doing anything else.
2. In a roasting pan, add the squash, aubergine and red peppers and 2 tbsp of the oil and toss to coat well.
3. Cook in the oven for about 40 minutes.
4. Meanwhile for the sauce in a food processor, add the onion, garlic, ginger and chili pepper and pulse till a rough paste is formed.
5. In a pan, heat the remaining oil and sauté the onion paste till the onions become tender.
6. Add the tomatoes and simmer for about 10 minutes.
7. Add the coconut cream and cook for about 5 minutes.
8. Add the cooked vegetables and chickpeas and cook till heated completely.

AROMATIC
Kenyan Curry

Prep Time: 45 mins
Total Time: 1 hr

Servings per Recipe: 8
Calories   348.6
Fat   5.1 g
Cholesterol   0 mg
Sodium   589.2 mg
Carbohydrates   68.2 g
Protein   11.6 g

Ingredients

2 large onions, finely chopped
2 tbsp vegetable oil
1 tsp cumin seed
1 tsp mustard seeds (the black kind, if possible)
8 medium potatoes, quartered
1 1/2 tsp fresh ginger, crushed
1 large garlic clove, minced and crushed
1 tbsp ground cumin
1 tbsp whole coriander seed, crushed
2 chili peppers
1/2 tsp turmeric
1 tsp salt

4 cinnamon sticks
6 cloves
4 oz. tomato paste
1/2 lb fresh green beans, trimmed
1/2 small cauliflower, broken into pieces
1 medium eggplant, cut into chunks
8 oz. green peas (fresh)
8 oz. leafy greens, chopped (small bunch, fresh, kale, spinach, collards, Swiss chard, etc.)
1 (15 oz.) can chickpeas, drained

Directions

1. Set your oven to 350 degrees F before doing anything else.
2. In a large, oven proof skillet, heat the oil on medium heat and sauté the onions, cumin seeds and mustard seeds till the onions become brown.
3. Add the potato pieces and the remaining spices and stir for several minutes.
4. In a bowl, mix together the tomato paste and 2/3 C. of the water.
5. Add the tomato paste mixture in the skillet and stir to combine.
6. Add the vegetables, one at a time and cook for about 1 minute between each addition.
7. Add the chickpeas and cook for about 1 minute.
8. With a lid, cover the skillet tightly.
9. Cook in the oven for about 45 minutes, stirring occasionally.
10. Once after the first 20 minutes. (Add more water if needed to prevent from the sticking)
11. Serve hot over the rice.

Cauliflower, Pumpkin and Lentil Curry

Prep Time: 15 mins
Total Time: 45 mins

Servings per Recipe: 6
Calories 261.7
Fat 4.2 g
Cholesterol 0 mg
Sodium 219.5 mg
Carbohydrates 45.5 g
Protein 13.9 g

Ingredients

1 tbsp vegetable oil
1 onion, finely chopped
500 g pumpkin, peeled and chopped into 3cm pieces
1 garlic clove, crushed
2 tsp curry powder
1 C. red lentil
1 liter vegetable stock
400 g chickpeas, drained
2 zucchini, cut into 3cm pieces
2 C. cauliflower florets
salt and pepper
chopped fresh coriander, to garnish

Directions

1. In a large pan, heat the oil and sauté the onion, pumpkin, garlic and curry powder for about 3 minutes.
2. Add the lentils and stock and bring to a boil.
3. Reduce the heat and simmer for about 5 minutes.
4. Add the chickpeas, zucchini and cauliflower and simmer for about 5 minutes.
5. Stir in the salt and pepper and remove from the heat.
6. Serve with a garnishing of the fresh chopped coriander.

PEAS, ZUCCHINI and Cabbage Curry

Prep Time: 25 mins
Total Time: 35 mins

Servings per Recipe: 6
Calories   81.8
Fat   2.6 g
Cholesterol   0 mg
Sodium   56.5 mg
Carbohydrates   13.1 g
Protein   3.6 g

Ingredients
1 tbsp vegetable oil
1 large white onion, sliced thin lengthwise
8 C. cabbage, slivered
1/4 C. chicken broth
2 medium zucchini, trimmed and sliced
1 1/2 tbsp curry paste
3/4 C. peas, frozen

Directions
1. In a large pan, heat the oil on medium-high heat and sauté the onion for about 1 minute.
2. Reduce the heat to medium and stir in the cabbage as will fit.
3. Add the chicken broth and add the remaining cabbage.
4. Cook, covered for about 10 minutes, stirring occasionally.
5. Stir in the zucchini and curry paste and reduce the heat to medium.
6. Cook for about 10 minutes.
7. Add the frozen peas and cook for about 5 minutes.
8. Stir in the salt and pepper.

Microwave Carrot Curry

Prep Time: 12 mins
Total Time: 25 mins

Servings per Recipe: 4
Calories	235.9
Fat	10 g
Cholesterol	0 mg
Sodium	665.8 mg
Carbohydrates	30.3 g
Protein	8.7 g

Ingredients

- 1 onion, sliced
- 2 tbsp green curry paste
- 3 C. carrots, sliced
- 1 (400 g) can chickpeas, drained
- 1 C. light coconut milk
- 1 tbsp lemon juice
- 1 tbsp soy sauce
- 1/2 C. nuts, chopped

Directions

1. In a large microwave safe casserole dish, place the onion and curry paste and cook on Very High for about 2 minutes.
2. Add the carrots, chick peas, coconut milk, lemon juice and soy sauce and cook on Very High for about 6-8 minutes.
3. Serve over the jasmine rice with a garnishing of the nuts.

ODIA
Veggie Curry

🍳 Prep Time: 35 mins
🕐 Total Time: 30 mins

Servings per Recipe: 4
Calories 298.8
Fat 18.2 g
Cholesterol 24.8 mg
Sodium 903.2 mg
Carbohydrates 31.9 g
Protein 6.5 g

Ingredients

- 3 tbsp oil
- 3 red chilies, seeded and chopped
- 6 cloves
- 4 cardamom pods, open at one end
- 1 inch cinnamon stick, broken up
- 2 bay leaves
- 1 onion, chopped
- 6 garlic cloves, chopped
- 1 tsp ground ginger
- 1 potato, in 1-inch cubes
- 1 carrot, sliced into rings
- 1 courgette, cubed
- 4 oz. green beans, in 1-inch pieces
- 1 green pepper, seeded and diced
- 1/2 tsp chili powder
- 1/2 tsp cumin powder
- 1 tsp coriander powder
- 1/2 tsp turmeric
- 140 g tomato paste
- 5 fluid oz. single cream
- 1 tsp salt
- 1 tsp garam masala
- 2 tbsp coriander (to garnish)

Directions

1. In a large pan, heat the oil and sauté the red chilis, cloves, cardamom, cinnamon stick and bay leaves till the bay leaves becomes golden brown.
2. Add the onion and sauté for about 2 minutes.
3. Reduce the heat and sauté the garlic and ginger for about 4 minutes.
4. Stir in all of the vegetables, chili powder, coriander powder, cumin powder, turmeric and 1/2 C. of the water and cook, covered for 15 minutes. (Add water if the mixture becomes too dry.)
5. Stir in the tomato paste and salt.
6. Reduce the heat to low and simmer, covered till the vegetables become tender.
7. Stir in the cream and garam masala and remove from the heat.
8. Keep aside, covered for about 2 minutes.
9. Serve over the plain boiled rice with a garnishing of the fresh chopped coriander.

Caribbean Country Curry

Prep Time: 30 mins
Total Time: 40 mins

Servings per Recipe: 4
Calories   352
Fat   5.1 g
Cholesterol   0.1 mg
Sodium   709.8 mg
Carbohydrates   71.8 g
Protein   11.2 g

Ingredients

- 1 C. basmati rice
- 1 C. cauliflower, chopped
- 8 oz. mushrooms, diced
- 2 green chili peppers, diced
- 1 C. pineapple, diced
- 2 medium onions, chopped
- 1 medium green bell pepper, chopped
- 1 tomato, chopped
- 1 C. tomato paste
- 3 tbsp curry powder
- 1 bouillon cube
- 2 C. boiling water
- 2 tsp marmalade
- 2 tsp tomato sauce
- 2 tsp olive oil
- salt and pepper
- paprika

Directions

1. In a pan, add 2 C. of the water and 1 c. of the rice and bring to a boil.
2. Reduce the heat and simmer, covered for about 15 minutes.
3. In a skillet, heat the oil and cook 1 of the onion, mushrooms, bell pepper, chili peppers for about 5-10 minutes.
4. In a bowl, dissolve the curry powder in 1 C. of the boiling water.
5. Add the curry powder mixture in the skillet and simmer for about 5 minutes.
6. In a bowl, crumble the bouillon cube in the remaining C. of the boiling water and stir to combine.
7. Add the tomato paste, marmalade, tomato sauce and bouillon cube mixture and stir well.
8. Stir in the cauliflower and pineapple chunks and simmer, covered for about 15 minutes.
9. In a bowl, add the remaining onion, tomato and paprika and toss to coat.
10. Serve the curry with a garnishing of the onion mixture.

TRADITIONAL
Indian Curry Paste

🍲 Prep Time: 5 mins
🕒 Total Time: 5 mins

Servings per Recipe: 1
Calories   225.4
Fat   10.4 g
Cholesterol   0 mg
Sodium   91 mg
Carbohydrates   33.3 g
Protein   8.8 g

Ingredients

2 1/2 tbsps coriander seeds, ground
1 tbsp cumin seed, ground
1 tsp brown mustard seeds
1/2 tsp cracked black peppercorns
1 tsp chili powder
1 tsp ground turmeric
2 crushed garlic cloves
2 tsps grated fresh ginger

3-4 tbsps white vinegar

Directions

1. Get a bowl, combine: coriander seeds, cumin seeds, mustard seeds, black peppercorns, chili powder, turmeric, cloves, and ginger. Stir the mix completely and evenly. Combine in the vinegar and begin to mash everything together into a paste.
2. Place your paste into a jar and seal the lid tightly. Your paste will stay fresh in the fridge for about 3 to 4 weeks.
3. Enjoy.

Green Curry Paste (Thailand Style)

Prep Time: 10 mins
Total Time: 10 mins

Servings per Recipe: 1
Calories   300.4
Fat   3.5 g
Cholesterol   0 mg
Sodium   2368.8 mg
Carbohydrates   71.1 g
Protein   7.5 g

Ingredients

- 1/4 C. chopped scallion
- 1/4 C. chopped fresh cilantro
- 2 tbsps minced garlic
- 2 tbsps grated fresh gingerroot
- 1 tbsp freshly grated lemon rinds
- 1 tbsp brown sugar
- 1-2 fresh red chilies or 1-2 green chili, minced
- 3 tbsps fresh lemon juice
- 1 tbsp ground coriander
- 1 tsp turmeric
- 1/2 tsp salt

Directions

1. Add the following your food processor: scallion, cilantro, garlic, ginger root, lemons / lime, brown sugar, chilies, lemon / lime juice, coriander, turmeric, and salt.
2. Process and pulse everything until it becomes a smooth paste.
3. Enjoy.

ENJOY THE RECIPES?
KEEP ON COOKING WITH 6 MORE FREE COOKBOOKS!

Visit our website and simply enter your email address to join the club and receive your 6 cookbooks.

http://booksumo.com/magnet

Made in the USA
Coppell, TX
04 December 2020